AF439439

MaleHeart

Stephen R. Andrew

Copyright © 2024 Stephen R. Andrew

Remember, this is one person's opinion.
Hold it very lightly.

ISBN: 979-8-8693-2548-8

Stephen R. Andrew
25 Middle Street
Portland, Maine 04101
www.hetimaine.org

Author's note

If you treat an individual ... as if he were what he ought to be and could be, he will become what he ought to be and could be.
Goethe

This pocket book looks deeply at how men can be emotionally oppressed in our culture, even allowing that men have economic power and are physically stronger than women and children. How we perceive male "hurt" makes a profound contribution to men's compulsions and obsessions, drug misuse and abuse or addiction, out of control sexual behavior, and other behavior problems. It affects men of all races and ethnicities. Young men are dying and/or killing others from this male socialization process. There must be something systematically in our culture that pushes men into the destructive behaviors of isolation, violence, and defense. What factors in our socialization process create the discomfort in men that leads them to compulsive and addictive behaviors.

Here I present a model of healing at the community level and at the individual level for all men.

Love in Action,

Stephen R. Richen

Acknowledgements

I would love to thank dearly the people who shaped me both personally and professionally: Wendy N., Carter R., Abby S., Donna H., Melissa G., Doug M., Kelley B., Doreen A., Mary C., John B., Bob K., Glenn C., Lacey S., Oliver B., Jayme V., Bob J., Linda J., David P., Marie S., Angelina M., Elizabeth M.L., Sarah S., Gabrielle R.T., Terri P., Michael N., Michael M., Rodney M., Jill F., Bill M., Terri M., Susan C., Alan L., David P., Steve B.S., Steven R., Tim A., Stefan, Dottie F., Tom C., Dino, Li B., friends in the MINT community and all of the people in our mutual aid support groups in the last 35 years, all of the donors to and board members of our nonprofit, Agape Inc., InnerEdge, and Dignity for People Using Opiates.

Hilary, Sebastian, Jeff S., Deborah S., Coral S., Joan A., John P., Robin C., Susan P., Michael P., Blaine H., Christine M., and the Kindred Spirits community.

Thank you Coffee by Design for supporting our podcast series Conversations in Compassion.

Thank you to ATTC: New England for your amazing support to people being trained & coached in Motivational Interviewing.

Finally, thank you to Danielle Sessler for her amazing editing on this book.

*If you talk to a man in a
language he understands,
that goes to his head.*

*If you talk to him
in his own language,
that goes to his heart.*

Nelson Mandela

MaleHeart

Growing up Male

How are men hurt and what is codependency (my definition: our adaptation to trauma)? Why do men need to gather with each other to soften the male oppression? Men supposedly have everything. We, men, have it all. I'm going to discuss how I perceive the word codependency and how it relates to the way men are hurt, and how at the crux of this are addictions, compulsions, and obsessions.

How we perceive male oppression makes a profound contribution to men's compulsions and obsessions, whether it be sex and love addiction, alcoholism, or other drug addictions. Today, men of all races and ethnicities are suffering and dying at a much higher rate from these diseases than women are. There must be something systematically in our culture that pushes men into destructive self-harming behaviors and diseases. What factors in our socialization process create the discomfort in men that leads them to obsessive and compulsive addictive behavior? I believe that there is a genetic factor, and for these diseases to take hold so broadly, they must be occurring within an environment that promotes and reinforces them. The male oppression is the systematic training done by the culture as a whole thru social messaging that creates a an emotional stuntedness.

What creates the discomfort in men so that they end up with codependency, alcoholism, and other drug use and misuse? Why is it that sixty percent of all the men in China now have a nicotine habit and only ten percent of the women do? Nation after nation these self-harmful behavior and other diseases happen to men.

When we are born, there's no evidence that there are inherent differences between men and women, in their ability to feel, their ability to think and figure things out, their ability to connect and be intimate, and their ability to be close in connection to other human beings. These abilities are universal, they are present at birth. We all can have the ability to be spontaneous, the ability to love and be loved, and we all have a strong yearning for power and control over our own destiny. None of these abilities and desires have been shown to be gender specific.

What happens is that little by little there are male socialization processes or "hurts", I'm going to call them traumas, that begin to chip away at men's self-esteem, self-worth, and their ability to be their own natural loving selves, their ability to be true to their emotional self. What are the kinds of traumas that happen directly to men, and what are the ways in which men get hurt?

What are these beliefs and messages men are socialized to accept that tear us from our natural selves? There is a myth that men are not supposed to have feelings and that in some way the feeling state within them is lost. That apart from anger, we're not supposed to feel. That the "good" man is strong, athletic, and physically expendable. That men are basically violent is a strong message in our culture and others. They must be protectors, providers, performers, and fixers. These beliefs are born in our culture and transmitted through media, literature, and the collusion of a society, ultimately tearing men away from their true core yearnings at rapid rates and causing powerful consequences to their internal and external worlds.

Male Violence

From the time boys are small, the idea of violence is implanted into them. Young boys who watch television, movies, and play video games see aggression between men represented. They might watch cowboy movies and observe all the men shooting at each other. How many movies have you seen with two women standing on either side of the town strapped with six guns ready to fire at each other? But from a very early age, boys are given toy guns, and when they use them against someone, who do they use them against? Another man. That has powerful implications. The notion of "kill or be killed" as a protective notion for others in the culture.

What must happen in your life for you to be convinced to kill another man? You'd have to devalue life. You'd have to think that life is expendable, or at least that the other person was expendable, and internally that you are also expendable. You would have to believe that there was something far more important than yourself, which could be your country, or protecting your family, but the notion would be carried in your head that your life was only as valuable as you were good at protecting and providing for others. So, men, instead of receiving the protection they needed, were made willing to sacrifice for other people. Society's message was, "If you want to keep the population going, you'll want to keep women safe, and use men as the warriors." And so, the more wars we had, the more we got involved in war, the more we had to train men to be willing to kill another. Men were given permission to hurt other people in order of protection.

You would then begin to make comparisons between men. Good guys versus bad guys. *Jack, there, is different from me. He acts out, he's not as good as me.* And so, we would begin to separate ourselves into good guys and bad guys, even on subtle comparative and competitive terms. Day in and day out, men are placed in competition with each other. They perceive situations as only win or lose, whether they are or not. Men constantly compare themselves to each other as if all resources are limited, and each other's situation is a zero-sum game. This way of thinking turns all men into potential enemies, not sources of support and connection. Life sources such as our own male friends and relatives, are not seen as compassionate witnesses, but as competitors. Creating a compulsion of isolation.

What would we have to do to convince each other we're the good guy, to convince the nation? Wouldn't we have to be rewarded in some way? Wouldn't we have to get some compensation for it? I don't mean in terms of economic compensation, although that is part of it, but we'd have to be given some compensation in terms of being hailed as a "hero". Therefore, we would be rewarded in terms of the process of killing in two ways. We are rewarded if we kill other men, and if we do it with bravery. And we are rewarded if we are killed in defending our nation or group. And what feeling in the repertoire of all feelings would you have to have at the forefront of your mind to accomplish this process? Hate/Rage.

Men being rewarded in the intense process of competition, where nothing is more important than winning, this kind of winning also implies losing. They are rewarded if they win over someone else, competitive sports, being a primary example. And men lose out on noncompetitive activities where everyone can win- these are generally drama, music, art to name a few. This sticks out more sharply. If you can imagine what our culture would look like if we intentionally encouraged collaboration, respect, empathy, compassion, and teamwork as priorities of a young man's life, instead of winning/competition.

Because when men lose, they feel ashamed, particles of shame, collected like dust on the soul, dimming their zest for life. A man's upbringing begins to separate himself internally between his inner good loving-self, and toxic shame - the suffering. The culture & institution rewards this competition through popular messaging, social media, conversations and in life, men's rewards are money and status/*power-over* another.

Men permit themselves to entertain only the emotions, anger and rage, that are consistent with the attitude to win, succeed, or achieve. How else can they accomplish these feats once a man begins to demand of himself success and the inner attitude to win at all costs? He must use aggression. Our whole culture thrives on the competitive aggression in boys and men. Boys are exposed to cruelty among one another, starting at the age of 10, the same age boys start paying attention to appearances and less to their families. This boyhood aggression lasts until he reaches the age of 15.   Until then its "boys being boys". The culture defends these actions while they're still minors, as if our culture gives young men permission to be aggressive/competitive. What comes of this permission is first poor impulse control and dealing with anger/ rage, and second, depression because holding onto the anger in every situation in which they perceive aggression or fear keeps their feelings and stories to themselves and causes isolation.

There are two schools of thoughts. One school of thought is men are inherently violent. Another school of thought is men are inherently lovers and they are trained to be violent. If the culture sees that men are inherently violent, then everything they do is perceived through that lens. Women are told they can have all the other emotions except anger. Men are told and systematically encourage they can only have anger/rage. All other emotions: sadness, fear, loneliness, joy and shame are unacceptable.

I think about this feeling of rage and how it fuels racism, sexism, poverty and all other forms of oppression. Once you begin to bore into rage, you can use it for any number of possibilities. For violence, for all kinds of sexism, for all kinds of violence against children, for oppression, for abuse to others. The chief emotion that comes out of that, and the only emotion I think is tolerable in terms of the external view, is anger/rage. Each of us, as men, are given permission on an ongoing basis to be mad. Now, how many of you are helpers? You have a male client walking through the door, and you've witnessed them focus on their addiction, which means that you've taken away the medication of his feelings. What are you going to see? You're going to see anger, or you're going to see depression, which is the opposites of anger, the holding on with dear life to anger/rage. So, you have two emotions looking at you. What happens next? Because if you receive support yourself and you are supporting other with men, then what happens is that as you're sitting there with this man and he is experiencing anger and/or depression, does your own anger/rage or depression (the pushing feelings down internally, all sadness, all loneliness, all fear, all shame, and of course joy) from your own maleness get ignited?

There are three main behaviors that men developed to manage their emotions: aggression, depression, and isolation. Fueling each of them in a feedback loop, this vicious cycle of aggression, depression, and isolation results in a cultural perception that men are insensitive and emotional, violent, physically, and sexually driven, and basically inhumane with others. Stuck (with power over) in a **right** position they often destroy their relationships.

Nurturing vs. Toughening Up

Boys, young men that are growing up today see more violence by the time they are ten years old than adult men have seen in their entire life, which means that they see four times as much violence portrayed in front of them. As a result of witnessing all this violence, systematically what begins to happen is that as males, codependency, their own way to manage the trauma whispers, sets in. I want you just to carry the notion of a definition of codependency. It is an adaptation of trauma, of suffering. It is the adaptation to extreme or rigid compulsive obsessive behavior; this adaptive behavior soothes the internal tension of the duality (the suffering and the desire to love well). It is the adaptation to what I call "hurts". In other words, as a little boy, when I grew up and watched my father and mother do what they did, which happened to be alcoholism, other drug misuse, addiction, codependency, and love & sex addiction. When I my watched them, my caregivers, I began to find my way. I had to find my way for survival of this internal discord. I had to adapt to certain patterns of behavior so that I could get as much as I possibly could (power and control over the destiny of my life) from that environment for my needs to be met. That adaptation is codependency. This codependency is a process, therefore, of me finding the whole, finding the place, the behaviors where I might get my attachment needs met. The attachment core needs of power and control, to love and to be loved, purpose/capable and connection/social capital.

Each boy, when you were born and somebody said you were a boy, they stopped touching you with kindness. And if they touched you, they slapped you or pinched you or poked you. They were trying to toughen you up. And in that process, you started to hunger for attachment needs. And you began to develop a pattern of self-harming behaviors and that were also useful to getting your attachment needs met. The statistics show that 27% of all men are sexually addicted in our culture. Now, a sexual and validation obsession, compulsion, addiction falling upon our gender of that kind of magnitude has a lot to do with this particular very basic attachment need to love and be loved and the need to be emotional constipated. We didn't get the core need fulfilled. If people were poking us and stopped holding us as much and touching us in a kind or loving way, then what happens at that moment is that we hesitate. And then in the locker room during our competitive training, when we gather, and we're given subtle permission now to oppress other people for power and we lack empathy for others, that's how we're going to get our needs met. And we have an underlying need to be touched. And of course, we can't touch each other because we've been taught that the violence of touching each other would not be healthy. So, what you see from each man when they get close to each other is anger, rage, and hatred.

These cultural messages are brought home to men when they are small boys and unable to protect themselves. They grow up watching fathers and mothers teach them about being a man, and what they receive are mixed messages. On one hand, they are taught to be strong and reliable, and on the other hand, they're left emotionalyl immature and stunted, insensitive, violent, and impulsive. After they were born and declared boys, they started being touched in less nurturing ways, and as they grew up even less and less, and then eventually less and less or only in a hard way, such as with a slap, pinch, or a poke. They were being taught to toughen up.

This approach to gender creates a deep, unsatisfying hunger for attachment and affection, a pattern developed over the course of boys and young men's formative years. It is no surprise that many men develop a huge journey to be touched. One of our culture's main sources of touch for men is sexuality, and it's become a conduit in which they seek to respond to the yearn and often become compulsive about touch. Data suggest that men are three times more likely to seek help for out of control, sexual compulsive behavior. A sexual compulsion rate of that magnitude occurring so distorted in one gender may reflect its social failure to meet boys and young men's very basic need for attachment. They want to be touched; they yearn for emotional attachment. And by the time boys become men they are living with a deficit that feels as if it can never be fulfilled.

Because all that is tolerable in the school yard between boys and the school yard of life that we live in is aggression. If you remember, it was competitive or it was violent. And in that process, we adapted our violence into a codependency of survival. We want to be touched; we want attachment. And so in our desire to be attached to people who were the figures in our lives, we found ourselves attaching consistently to women. Our elementary school teacher was generally a woman. Even the babysitter that parental figures brought in to watch us, was traditionally a woman. Every figure in our lives that showed us any kind of nurturance, any place that we could look out into the screen and develop our own identity, was typically a woman. And really, codependency is delayed identity.

But we couldn't adapt because we knew we weren't ourselves women. There was the feeling of, how do we do this? What are we about? What is our identity? And the only thing we saw were men who were out there trying to provide, trying to make it. And if it was anything like my relationship to my father, it was very far away. You see, my father was stricken by the disease of alcoholism. So, he was very far away.

So, I took on the notion that there must be something wrong with me because I can't develop an identity like a female could. And the men in my life were very distant. And in fact, if we just spent a little bit of time moving our bodies close together, we'd notice feelings in us would come up, feelings of homophobia, of hatred, and anger. So, any male who did try to develop us, whether it was a coach or a person in our neighborhood who tried to get close to us, they would/could get labeled.

So, you needed to take a protective distance from the boys. I want you to imagine if a woman walks into a room and there's a bunch of girls playing and they're having a great time, and a woman walks over and hugs the girls one by one, would you have any difficulty with that? Do you think society would have any difficulty? In contrast, if a group of young men are playing with trucks and cars and banging them together, running around the room with all their energy, and a man comes in the room and he starts hugging the boys, and our society was able to look down upon this scene, what notion would come up?

Society would brand this man as being too loving, too sexual, and violating little boys' boundaries. It is no wonder that men develop the disease of codependency. It is no wonder that males develop an ongoing basis at the rate of two to one, if not three to one, the disease of alcoholism and other drug addiction.

Let's return to the fact that there's no evidence for fundamental differences between men and women at birth. Both need to be loved, both need to feel capable and powerful, both need to be connected to others. The key to a healthy mental and physical health is connection. In contrast, the social script that men must be too aggressive, too sexual, unable to show any emotion other than anger/rage, and incapable of being caregivers to our children, produces a constant stream of male low self-worth and self-esteem. Instead of toughening men up, it leaves them vulnerable to anything that can ease the pain. This is a set up for compulsive, obsessive, and addictive behaviors.

Male Obsessions, Compulsions and Addiction

Compulsive/Addictive behavior can numb the internal emotional pain felt through the oppression of growing up from boy to man, especially during the age of the gauntlet of cruelty, ages 10 to 15. If men do not transform this pain, they will transmit it onto themselves creating self-harm and/or onto people they love and others into the community. Men develop the dis-ease of compulsions and addiction at three times higher rate than women. And after years of messages, "Don't feel," "Don't trust other boys," Don't get too close to other boys," after years of not having had basic core attachment needs met and being encouraged to buy into the attitude that girls and young women are objects for pleasure, and/or emotional nurturance. Boys and men live in the contradiction, the duality with their true self in the world of the oppression, suffering and "hurt", deeply injured around their emotional intelligence and their ability to be compassionate for self and others.

Most men have some level of underlying pain because of working so hard to do it *right*, to be perceived as a "good" person, a "good" man, and since we generally do not have an internal resource to repair the "hurt", we find something external, something manly and acceptable to repair and medicate our emotional immaturity.

It is no wonder because after you've been oppressed/injured in our heart and our soul, after you haven't had our basic attachment core needs met, you keep getting "hurt". Let's imagine for a moment that you walked every day of your life, and you got hit right here on the shoulder, Right there? Right there again? You just got hit. And the way you got hit was just by simple phrases like, "Don't cry little boy." Okay? You just get hit. "Be a man. Be tough, be a man." Okay? Weren't you encouraged to be physical, to win? Weren't you encouraged to have lots of energy? Wasn't that good for you, huh? But then they put you in a classroom and told you to shut up and sit down, juxtaposed exactly against the energy they told you to have. So, all these things began to happen to you, right? You got hit every single day. "Don't feel, don't trust, don't get close to other boys. Make sure you hit/push back at somebody. Make sure you're aggressive. Make sure you're strong, right?" Weren't you told to be aggressive/to win? Was it more likely to be aggressive? Was it good to be gentle if you were a 10-year-old boy? You know, you kind of liked other people. You told them they were nice. Was that what you were told? No, but that's our general nature. That's our general nature and the human experience. We are gentle, empathic human beings. So, you get hit every day, with messages incongruent with our natural humanness. What would happen after a while? Wouldn't you move your shoulder out of the way, would your start forming to adapt? Wouldn't you move it to not experience the "hurt"? you would still have to exist. So, now you'd walk around with a slump, and this stuff kept happening to you. And because you were isolated, now you see how men could get isolated, accurately pursue loneliness because there's no way we could connect with other men or women. We try to connect with women and what happens to us because we think through our pesky ego because of a man's need to be **right** and they feel the lack of compassion, lack of heart, they can't get too close to us. We live in an emotional prison believing we are connecting. And most men today growing up are living in single parent families. Who's the single parent? Women. So, the culture continues to do this, and here's this boy child now walking like this in the mind and not the heart, the emotions. All of us men walking like this, we have adapted ourselves in terms of our own version of codependency. We've adapted ourselves like this. And then we get into life, and somebody says, "Stand up for the rumbling of those emotions and values." And you say, "no thank you very much". Those hurts. Every time I stand up, every time I am vulnerable, I get hit.

So, you isolate yourself. You isolate yourself because you know there's something wrong with this, and you don't want anybody to see the pain. You must walk, talk, and think like this. So, what do you do? You adapt. You slide down into your depression, you get aggressive. So, it doesn't draw so much attention to your vulnerability. You try to succeed, you try to provide, you try to get involved in as many things as possible. You keep chasing because something's wrong here. And I want to tell you that when a teenage boy picks up a drink, and he has been hugged 400 times less by the time he's 10, when a little boy has been given the kind of stimuli of violence time after time after time, when a little boy is told that he better like math and science because that's a male thing to like time after time, and he doesn't like it, he knows in his heart he doesn't like it. He wants to draw. And that continues to happen, that when he becomes an adolescent boy and he picks up a drink for the first time in his life, he'll have finally gotten rid of that tension of the internal discord.

He doesn't feel the pain. No longer can anybody "hurt" him. He's gotten a glow right in his body. And you know what I mean? If you've had the addiction/compulsion, a glow right in there. So, it's a power and control. You are not powerless anymore over the "hurt" or somebody pounding you in the shoulder. You feel powerful for the moment if you put a little white stuff in your nose, place a needle of heroin in your veins. And boy, I tell you, that's all you want- power over that internal trauma, the injury, the "hurt".

You could care less about history because when you're an adolescent boy, history lasts 48 hours. That's it. And so, for a moment, just for a moment, you feel okay, you feel powerful, and it has created an imprint in the brain, this is how I can be alone and soothed. And all their peers have kind of got you to that situation anyways because they've kind of encouraged you to be external, not internal, you know? Can you imagine walking down the corridor of that school building and saying, "I want to meditate to quiet my internal anxiety." No way. In fact, if you ever told anybody that you had any dreams about meditating or just getting a sense of yourself, then what would happen is that you would be called a "sissy". Something's wrong with you, you are weak! You will be isolated even further. Think about the ways that men are isolated.

You see, compulsions/addiction to me equals isolation. The process of addiction is isolation, disconnection. So, at first you might be socializing, and, after a while, it gets more and more isolated. And you know, we were taught as young boys on an ongoing basis to isolate ourselves anyway. You see, the way that we were isolated is that when we had feelings, we were told to go away and process them in isolation, unless it was anger. If you had little internal boundaries with your anger and it got bigger than the person near you got frighten then you would be given shame for your rage. External compulsions are less harmful then injuring others, especially women and children.

Imagine for a moment, just imagine a young boy coming into the house and he's crying because he has just gotten "hurt" outside. He fell out of a tree, and he hurt his arm and he's coming inside. Some of the messages that will happen to that little boy are, "Stop crying, stop crying, shake it off. You'll be alright. **Be tough."**

We are told that we have a different feeling structure than women. If that same girl came in with that same arm, she wouldn't be told, "shake it off." She'd be encouraged to feel it. And we were told that we had a different feeling structure systematically, a little bit at a time. Nobody stood up and said, "Excuse me, you're a boy, you have a different feeling structure," and you see who oppresses men.

You know, men would not oppress anybody if we had any feelings left. There would be no way that we would oppress people of color. There would be no way we would oppress anybody who was gay.

There would be no way that we would oppress women if we could feel the full rainbow of emotions. And men's' feelings were taken away systematically. I want to say this very clearly. It is true that men oppress women. That is true. That is a truism. And there are lots of ramifications in that. But the other truism is that men and women together oppress men's emotions. It happens, and the way we get hurt is because society condones it. And it condones this on an ongoing basis through the image and messages. We are socialized- taught on a personal level by our caregivers, relatives, teachers, people we love and trust- they are the shapers of expectations, norms values, roles, rules, all models' ways to be in our hopes and dreams. Institutions and culture reinforced and bombarded with messages on a conscious and unconscious levels. And the way it condones it is first, and these are just some of the ways, and for instance, most men are told on an ongoing basis that their self-esteem is connected to their work, economic security. Anybody feel that how much money you make or what you do, is what comprises your self-esteem? I do. I am riddled by the dis-ease of workaholism.

I am riddled by it, because the one thing my father did during his alcoholism is that he went to work every day. He was a chronic stage alcoholic, tripping over his feet, ending up at a civil service job. That's the only way he could have kept the job. and in his mind, he wasn't an alcoholic because he went to work every day. Men are told to work, to provide, to perform we were told from all the pictures that we are supposed to leave the teepee and go out and hunt. And how many days would we leave until we found what we needed? And so, we would provide and leave. And when we left, did we go with a whole pack of others? Generally, we went alone. We did not travel in a "pack". And the natural essence of all human beings is to travel in packs, social capital. The great Indian warrior said, we are all like wolves. We travel in packs. We want to travel in packs because the basic essence of us is to love and to be loved. But if we end up traveling alone all the time in our own journeys, then what happens is that breeds isolation. And anytime you're in contradiction with your true self, that creates hurt. And since we have no way to repair the hurt, we must find something external that is acceptable for us to utilize, to repair the hurt. And what becomes acceptable? What becomes acceptable for us to repair the hurt?

Take a mate. Not only take a mate and take them as a hostage. And if by chance, that mate starts to winder away or doesn't like what we're about in our emotional intelligence, what are we supposed to do? Dump it and get another one? Quick, move it. We're riddled by love addiction. One, after the other, after the other. We don't know how to connect. Remember that there is no communication between a male and a female existent in our present culture. When you both sit down and start talking about, "this is the way I was hurt" maybe then, but it's not within the same repertoire. It's not within the same mindset. You know, we speak two different languages, and it sounds the same. Women say to us, "feel," when what they really mean is "feel pain, feel sadness." So, when we go to feel, which is our first emotion that will pop up? Anger. And what will they do with the anger? Cover it up. Tell it to get out of here.

Because women are told by society, "don't ever be angry."

So, they're saying, "Feel." And then when men do feel, women say, "Don't do that." So, we have this whole dilemma of the communication process. And so, what we do is shove our feelings inside. See, behind the anger is the sadness. And the only way that you are going to be able to help men is to allow their anger/rage to be present to really be present so that you can see the hurt, suffering and the sadness, the grief of being systematically "hurt" day by day by day. And so, the only way that women are going to find an intimate relationship with men is to give us permission to feel grief, shame, and joy. And that probably won't happen because women experience men's anger/rage and it comes out as emotional violence and rape, and they're not interested in seeing our anger, because it involves their oppression. So, men are going to have to gather with one another, because it is a place where we can communicate, learn empathy, and connect deeply with the male oppression.

It will be scary the vulnerability, and it's one of the reasons most men haven't done the work. And if you're in a relationship with somebody, you need to know that you're going to be a witness. You are going to see each other's anger/rage, and you need to be comfortable with that person's anger and set clear boundaries to the rage which is probably going to trigger yours. And you need to have a place to release your own anger in dialogue. If you are in a loving relationship with another man of any type, you're going to see his anger/rage. And when you see his anger, you need to be open to understanding that that is part of the socialization, that is part of the hurt. It doesn't mean it has to hurt you; it doesn't mean that it must be placed upon you. And the normal ways that we can figure out to contradict when we've been hurt, in pain are generally around not having feelings, being overburdened, being over responsible, being providers, protectors and perform on the outside of self. We need to give men the permission to **rest**.

Now it is okay for us to **rest**. We're over fatigued, we're stressed. We generally have underlying depression because we've been working so hard to do it right, to catch that vision of the warrior. We give you permission to stop running for it. Be in touch and gather the possibility of connecting with your true self. What's been frozen the most are men's hearts. You see, there are some gifts of being male, and one of these gifts is that we're willing to take the lead. We're willing to challenge to unknown for others. The problem has been that in that process, we have turned away from leading from and with our hearts, our emotions. The oppression has stolen systematically the male heart, it was taken away. And if we are open to the possibility, we can thaw our hearts and get back to leading from this open place. **_LOVING WELL!_**

Male Gathering vs. Isolation

Every man that you approach from here on, I want you to know that within him is innate goodness. No matter what their record says, or how "out of touch" the culture has this man as being. They want to love well, to have purpose, to experience being capable, to have social capital/belong.

Just carry that notion into every relationship that this is somebody that's been hurt, their soul undamaged has been injured. And that underneath that hurt is always innate goodness. Even if you look at the fact that our prisons are filled 20 times more with men than there are women. Men are taught from a very early age to be violent. That is one of the hurts. And you might say that because of this, men need to be isolated. My sense isn't that these are men who need to be isolated, my sense is that these are men that have been hurt and need to be connected the loss in the injury is compassion and radical acceptance of another.

Our tendency as people, as men is to go to women with our emotions. Has anybody ever noticed? It's a desperate desire to be safe. It comes from a wonderful place. Now to contradict that, just for a moment, I'm going to ask you, to begin to make a challenge to yourself, to take that same that emotionality and go towards other men. That's not to say that you can't have intimate relationships with women. I ask you to just for the moment to balance your existence to include the other half of humanity into your deepness. Any of you who are involved in helping, I challenge you now to begin to make some of your codependency care just for men to connect to men. And you know, I might be considered an outsider, but having done codependency support for men, I can see the richness, I can see the language of caring, I can see the potential of creating a safe compassionate place for men to talk about some of the concepts, some of their hurts, injuring they experienced we've discussed here in this book. Talk about the oppression without judgment.

The power and the possibility of what it means for men to have a place to explore getting down to the level of the fear, the abandonment, and the hurt of not having any kind of compassionate male role-modeling.

How can we go within ourselves to be courageous? Men are spiritual creatures. You see why we're so spiritual is that we've been isolated to a point where the only place we could go is within to our spirituality. We had to bring some fantasy in to survive, riddled with compulsions and /or addiction, riddled with no closeness, riddled with no attachment, no ability to meet our core needs, riddled with not being touched in ways that soothe our cells. Out of this has come the addictions and the compulsions. We need to gather as men, as part of our codependency care. I also challenge you, as part of the strategies of what's next, is that we need to be mentors for our little boys. And I mean that in two ways. One, we need to make a commitment as men to the boys out there in the world. And I do that with tears in my eyes because they really do need us, desperately.

I notice from the high school aged boys and men that I supported, that they're so alone and they're so desperate. You know, they don't walk into my office to talk about their feelings. They just don't. 75% of my practice is women. Does that mean that men are more secure, happy, loving, and connected? No, it means that we're isolated even more so. Our little boys, the ones inside of ourselves and the ones out there in the world, desperately need us to develop our emotional identities. When we offer a program these days, we find that they're built with 70% girls and 30% boys. Whether it be a program in a middle school or elementary school, we need to be intentional about choosing to leave open slots and encourage the males to be a part. They won't reach out, they don't know how to take initiative. They only know isolation.

50% of the boys now will grow up in a family where there's only a single mother. We are going to see the same compulsions and addiction. Underlining this obsessive, compulsive addictive behaviors will be that if you're not connected, you will drink, use some obsession. And compulsion, drinking will kill men. We don't have to go to war anymore. We're dying in our own homes.

We're dying as a male species, as a gender. Our life expectancy is 10 or 15 years shorter because we're male, no other reason, not because of cigarettes or drugs, no other reason. Maleness, what does that tell you?

When you hear that conversation that men don't have feelings, I'd like you to contradict that. I'd like you to say to another woman or man, "That's not true." I would like you to say, "In fact, men have within them the whole range of feelings, joy and love, happiness, fear, shame, and sadness, hurt and pain. They have all of them and they've been systematically hurt. And because of the lack of disclosure about this oppression, I know you do not understand how that happened. And I understand when I say that I might need to bring up your anger/rage of your oppression that we have been safe, non-judgmental placed to do the work of vulnerability. We understand that that need to gather. I want you to know that the truism, the true self of all men, is that they're feeling/emotional creatures. And that when each of us begins to change our attitude about how we perceive men, the perception of how men are perceived changes in our culture.

Male Perception

Here is a list that I put together, not completely comprehensive, about how we view men in this culture. Some of the words might be brutal to the soul:

Lonely, depressed, angry, avoidant, moody, desperate, numb, alienated, hopelessness, violent, controlling, exploitive, workaholic, substance abuser, drunk, sexually inappropriate, sexually compulsive, other difficulties with sexual intimacy, other addictions, or obsessions, avoids commitments, withdrawn, cannot get close, stressed out, neglected, unable to know his needs. poor self-esteem, lack of vision when it comes to intimacy, no sense of purpose. inability to relax, inability to have fun or play. critical, powerful, power hungry, competitive, and lacking cooperation.

Do these sound-like men?

What I'm asking you to do is to take those notions and see that none of them are true. They're not true. These are the messages that you were given, of what men should be like because of the male oppression. Every time that's put out there as a notion, you are being hurt as a male. When I put it upon you, the judgement is a form of violence, when I put it upon someone else, another male is hurt/injured. When we allow these messages to continue to happen to men, we are hurting/injuring men, as well as all of humankind. And I challenge you to not let these messages continue in our culture and to teach men and boys about these messages, to uncover the suffering. When you see a man sitting across from you - a friend, a family member, someone in relationship or your sponsor relationship - he is none of those things. He may behave in some of those ways, but he is none of those things. And I ask you with all your vigor never to allow yourself to box men into this corner, hopefully choose empathy and compassion. When you see that happen to a man, I ask that you to let go and encourage people not to see men in their life in that way of their oppression.

How could men feel fully loving, fully cooperative, fully compassionate, full of the ability to have empathic understanding, to connect deeply to others? The question is the suffering or loving fully. That's the trauma adaptation that we took will cause men to be defensive, aggressive and/or avoidant, isolated. That's the codependency, that's the dis-ease that men had to take to survive. We can qualify it by saying this is how one had to behave to survive - it's not necessary today. It may be that you continue to survive, it's not necessary for me to continue to enhance that message to yourself. You may still need some of that to survive, to protect the self. I'm not questioning that on the streets for males it might be necessary, it still hurts. I am questioning that when you get down into an individual relationship with a man, that you don't have to keep the systematic messaging happening. It's placed upon men, and it doesn't need to be there.

Let's take fatherhood for example. What's the notion of fatherhood in our society? Here are just a few of the ideas that come to mind, and I'd like for you to take some time to personally reflect on this question.

- Provider
- Good role model
- Protector

- The one who is ultimately responsible
- Spiritual leader
- Disciplinarian. How many people were told, "Wait until dad comes home?"
- Person who teaches us how to fix the world
- Person who teaches you how to play sports with team in mind
- The person who teaches boys how to treat women and other oppressed groups

Just for a moment, I'd like you to go inside and think about your own father. Look inside and think of your dad and think of the gifts he gave you. What are some of the things you saw? Take some time to reflect with yourself on this teaching.

I believe we were passed a toolbox by our dad. And in the toolbox were all his capabilities. And that toolbox was shiny. It was all nicely done. It was done with as much compassion, love, and nurturance that he was given in his life. Totally given to you. Now if there's anything like my toolbox, when I finally opened it up and went into a relationship with another human being, I found out I had a left-handed monkey wrench. And I have never been left-handed. I found out that none of the tools worked, but I didn't know that when I was given the box, I just took what I needed and tried to use it. And the quest for each of us as males is to understand our maleness comes from our fathers, the men in our lives, and their fathers. And then placed on top of that maleness is all the things that we were taught from our society, the community, and the people around us. But deep within that, is the maleness of the father and the quest to have a father. In my case, I drifted out into the community to find a dad. I spent most of my life trying to find fathers. At 39 years old, I was still looking for a father.

And I'd have a love-hate relationship with most authority because I both loved my dad, and I hated my dad' dis-ease. And today I must look at every relationship in a mirror of my relationship to my father. And I encourage you to do the same because that is your closest identity in your life. Your mother gave you another view of the world, each gender having tasks in our development. Even though she might've been closer in your life, that father was the identity of the same gender that you really tried to identify with, the strongest you tried to connect your heart to. If that person was riddled by the dis-ease of codependency, compulsions, and addiction, then when you tried to plug into his heart, it wasn't there. And if you are anything like me, you spent less of your life chasing with your heart, but instead trying to plug into someplace. You know what I found to plug in? I tried to plug into women for a while, see if that would work and that would last. And some of us have been plugging into other men and racing through. And now we're riddled with the dis-ease because we've been in our love, compassion, trying to plug in on an ongoing basis to multiple relationships, both female and male, trying to plug our heart into another man desperately, to meet the need of our masculinity.

It is no wonder that we have the dis-ease of pornography, obsessions, compulsions, alcoholism, other drugs. It is no wonder that we have the dis-ease of love and sexual addiction. I'm not baffled by it. I can tell you, based on what's happened to me as a man, it's no wonder that I'm love addicted, sex addicted, riddled by other dis-eases. The way I introduce myself now in the 12-step program is, "Hi, my name's Stephen and I'm addicted to everything that helps me not feel, not trust another."

I am. This heart has been looking for some place to plug into all its life. All it must do is for a moment feel good. That's all it must do. Just give me a moment, a moment. If you want to think about the way men really are. Every male is fully male, filled with suffering and hopes and dreams. You know how we were told that we must chase our maleness, our warriorhood. We must do certain things to prove that you are male. That's not true. We are already inherently male; you can **rest** now. Our purpose is to create a sense of androgyny. We can just all give a big sigh and think about how difficult it is - that concept and that notion to hold, to be androgynous. Every male is fully male. Isn't some committee jumping into your head that says, "Not quite yet, I haven't done it quite yet. I haven't made $500,000 yet. I haven't gotten it just yet." Every male is completely, and I mean completely good, whole, innocent, pure, without exception.

Anybody thinking to themselves of any exceptions? There must be a couple expectations, right? There are some guys sitting in prison, and we think to ourselves that they're not pure and innocent. I mean, they might maintain that they're innocent. You know the guy that's sexually abused the entire neighborhood. He is not pure and innocent. He's not whole, is he? I challenge you just for a moment to hold that notion of him being whole - because what I would say about that male, not to relinquish him from the responsibility of their behaviors, I'm not trying to do that. I'm not trying to say that his behavior is correct. I'm trying to say underneath the hurt, the injury of systematic messaging of the culture of that man holds this notion that every man you approach from now on is completely good, innocent, pure, and whole. Without exception, you can hold them responsible for their behavior. I encourage you to do so. The notion of kind boundaries helps men process their suffering. The home of that defensive, aggressive, rage filled, isolated, avoidant behavior lacks empathy for another is to "hurt" the other and is what they had to do to survive to get their basic needs met, power, love, connection.

We're all "hurt", We are all suffering and I choose distinctively to change that word. I don't see anything wrong in the view of another man. I see that we've been hurt, we've been socialized, we've been pushed, we've been poked in such a way that we have developed certain behaviors to adapt to that hurt, that injury. It's time to release that hurt. It is time to develop compassionate witnesses in your life. And that will take some focus because we didn't get it overnight. The awareness is first- What happened? Be courageous to say your truth without shaming self and others. Then, develop the skills of empathic understanding, compassion, we didn't wake up one day, and they said "Here, here's the boy, man, hurt it." What happened to us was that we got hurt systematically by culture and the community institutions. Every male is completely powerful and intimate. And I mean that in cooperation, not in competition. Every male is completely powerful, loving, lovable, and brilliant by nature. **By nature, every man is tender and nurturing. *Without exception.*** You know how men are told that we don't nurture children? Anybody ever heard that? That we don't know how to hold them right? That we don't know how to cuddle them. We don't know how to get them close to us. We're not very nurturing people. Ever been told that, ever heard that about men?

That's the systematic current, and it's not true. It is true that biologically we're not there right now of infancy to provide a particular substance. That's it. Where it ends. We absolutely can be as nurturing as women, to hold, love, and to nurture. We are fun. We are silly, we're playful, we're caring, we're deeply feeling people, deeply. We're sexual, we're compassionate. We're sensual. We're kind, gentle. Those are absolutely the true notions.

Antidotes

If I treat an individual as he is, he will stay as he is, but if you treat him as if he were what he ought to be, and could be, he will become what he ought to be, and could be.~ Goethe

There are a series of things that we can do to provide antidotes to the conditioning and socialization of men to open their hearts:

♥ The first thing men need to do is to develop some questions and answers around their relationships to their fathers. To look at the hurts and the trauma whispers- the thought is, "I don't matter", "I am not loveable", "the world is not to be trusted" when a hurt and trauma is stuck inside the body of an individual man, what happens to it is that it will become stored vital energy. And that energy will have to work itself out. Men are hurt in so many ways, what happens is that they work it out through the only pathway that's allowable often internal-depression, aggression. And that's violence. The trauma hides inside the cells. What we need to do now is to help men recognize, evoke the story - listen deeply with empathy and acceptance where they've been hurt. Invite the courageous vulnerability in hopes that they will be heard, believed, seen, and valued.

♥ As a man, one of the supportive options is to encourage men to speak freely on how they've been hurt and how they're going to contradict it within the bounds of supporting them. Empathy is the antidote to toxic shame. For instance, you also need to speak within your relationship with them about maybe the feelings they have about being close to you because there's homophobia (remember we are not to be close as men to each other, as a injury we suffered) in the individual relationship between you and another man. It's there a possible intimacy. And the quest is, can you recognize it, the hurts of the oppression in support? Can you be comfortable with the hurts because they are like our own? Can you deal with the PAIN? And if you can, you need to bring it up, challenge yourself to speak to the oppression.

Because the closer they get to each other, the more hurt is going to come up, to be released. Relationships are a laboratory for the place of "hurt". The closer I get to you, the more the "hurt" is going to come to the surface. You must be willing to understand that the way it's going to come out is good. Generally, it's going to come out in an angry/defensive way. It's going to try to criticize you as a support person, push you away, get you to push them away. It'll do any number of behaviors to get rid of the vulnerability. So, what I'm suggesting here is that you see the hurt, the suffering. You coach them to talk about the hurts.

♥ Next is you help them to resolve the grief. We need to do our grief work. The grief work is very central to what we didn't get. What we didn't get, in most cases, was a well-connected, cooperative, loving mentors, father - having nothing to do with that individual. Remember that individual man was completely good, doing the best they can do right? Completely loving and suffering. They got hurt in such a way that they couldn't deal with the closeness of being close to us. So, there's a great deal of grief, sadness that separates us. We need to contradict it by questioning, by asking for males to be close through the skillfulness of empathy and compassion.

♥ If you are involved in the helping or supporting a young man/men and men in your life, I challenge you to be in a collective of men, both formally and informally. We need compassionate witnesses. And I'll share with you a little bit about our men's mutual aid support group. And within these confines, there's lots of discussion about our past trauma, hurts of our lives. Our agreement is that the discussion will be about what it's like to be a man. There be no unsolicited advice. That's our topic is our present moment, and we receive empathy and compassion from each other. Now, that can go in any number of ways, that's a very rich topic, self-injury. We'll start to break the isolation that equals compulsions, addiction, and dis-ease. At any time, you can get together with other men, just encourage a little bit of their heart to ripple out into the world, not from a place of competition, and from a place of cooperation and connection.

I ask men to call for an action where we no longer must be responsible for society, it's a shared responsibility. Where we no longer must be burdened by making all the decisions, it's a shared decision. I encourage you to be comfortable with ambiguity, the sweet duality of the human soul. We think we must decide. I ask you to hesitate on making most of the decisions just for a little bit, take a breath. As men, we were expected to be able to fix it all. Just encourage the men in your life to be the spiritual warriors that they really are.

And let me just end this sweet timely tiny book in a couple of ways.

First, I would like to end with the thought about spiritual warriors. Each of us as a male is a spiritual warrior. We will be asked of us to take a quest, a vision quest, to gather our toolboxes of what we've been taught and go out into the world with other braves men, and together find our vision of loving well. I encourage every male to do the same, go on the quest to be powerful, be capable, to be loving. We never become intimate with women and children in our lives without the ritual by your deep friendships with other men, leaving our boyhood oppression into our manhood. We need to do that ritual and continue to the end of our lives, invite the into-me-I see (Intimacy) of the male heart. And for every boy we meet, we need to create rituals for them to move from their boyhood into their manhood with other boys, young men understanding the oppression, the skills of empathy and compassion. Create rituals for yourself as a spiritual warrior. Warrior does not mean to kill any longer. Warrior means to go for it, to learn the vulnerability of bravery. You can have it all. Not at the expense of anybody. Just in your **MaleHeart**.

Lastly, I'd like to share this prayer and affirmation with you that we speak at all our men's groups that we host. May you recite this within your own practice, with groups, with friends, with family members, or just within your own heart.

As a man, I promise to be proud to be a man who will seek the closeness and connection of every man, of every race, age, nation, and class. I will permit no slander or disrespect or blaming of any man for the hurts that have been placed upon them through the process of oppression and trauma. I will seek to restore emotional safety to all men and be a witness to the release of the cruel hurts. I will fight to end and eliminate the burden of boys and men over responsibility, over competition, and overwhelming fatigue. I will cherish my birthright as a boy and a man and I will cherish being good, intelligent, courageous, empathetic, powerful, loving male human, I promise.

ABOUT THE AUTHOR

Stephen R. Andrew LCSW, LADC, CCS is a storyteller, consultant, community organizer and trainer who maintains a compassion-focused private practice and facilitates weekly men's, coed, women's, and Motivational Interviewing learning groups. He provides coaching and training domestically and internationally for social service agencies, health care providers, substance abuse counselors, criminal justice, and other groups on motivational interviewing, supervision, ethics for caring services professionals, men's work, and the power of group work. Stephen lives in Portland, Maine with his sweet wife Hilary, and is the proud father of Sebastian.

Making it happen is our commitment to the world ~50% of our profits will go to the (not- for- profit), AGAPE Inc., dedicated to providing support services and education to create compassionate solutions that strengthen our communities.

www.agapemaine.org

9 7 9 8 8 6 9 3 2 5 4 8 8